The Not-So-Scary Scarecrow

Written by Robin Bloksberg · Illustrated by Dan Clifford

One day Mark planted a garden in his backyard.

The garden grew.

A hare came to eat from the garden. A crow
came to eat from the garden.

Mark needed a scarecrow for his garden.

He made hair from yarn. He made a nose from
tree bark. He used a pair of marbles for eyes.
He gave the scarecrow clothes.

Mark worked hard on his scarecrow.

Then he asked his friends to come see it.

"It's a nice scarecrow, but it's too fat! It won't scare the crows away!" said Carl.

10

So Mark took some straw out.

"It's a nice scarecrow, but it's too thin! It won't scare the crows away!" said Mary.

12

So Mark stuffed the straw back in.

"It still isn't very scary," said Artie.

"I don't care!" said Mark. "I worked hard on this scarecrow. I like it just the way it is!"

But so did the crows! They came to Mark's garden. They sat on his scarecrow.

And they scared Mark away.

16